BEANSTALK'S BASICS FOR PIANO

TECHNIQUE BOOK
PREPARATORY
LEVEL A

BY CHERYL FINN AND EAMONN MORRIS

© 2001 by The Willis Music Company
All Rights Reserved. Any reproduction, in whole or in part, of any aspect of this publication including music, illustration or text is an infringement of copyright law and is subject to prosecution. Do not copy.
www.willismusic.com

FINGER GYM EVENTS

Wiggle Warm-Up Right!	3
Wiggle Warm-Up Left!	4
Weight Lifting	5
Bicycle Race	6
Doing Free Weights	7
Walking on Tippytoes	8
Playing Copy Cat!	9
Spinning Around!	10
High Stepping	11
Wheel Barrow Race!	12
Walking Fingers	13
Finger March	14
Stretching	15
Soccer Try-Outs!	16
Soccer Game Warm-Ups	17
Baseball Try-Outs!	18
Baseball Game Warm-Ups	19
Volleyball Try-Outs!	20
Volleyball Game Warm-Ups	21
Swim Team Try-Outs!	22
At The Swim Meet!	23
Playing Frisbee	24
Rope Climbing	25
Soccer Drill	26
Walk & Rest!	27
Hoola Hoops!	28
Skipping Stones	29
Twirling Around	30
Egg & Spoon Relay	31
Water Relay	32

PARENTS, STUDENTS AND TEACHERS! WELCOME TO THE FINGER GYM!

The performance of daily technical exercises is an essential part of piano training. Like an athlete, the pianist cannot perform to full capability without proper physical conditioning.

Beanstalk's Basics for Piano Technique takes the student's fingers into the gym every day for a series of exercises and games taken right out of gym class! These **Finger Gym** workouts not only improve finger dexterity, independence, control, stamina, hand position, style and musicianship, but also help to stimulate musical imagination.

Beanstalk's Basics for Piano Technique uses colorful stickers to reward a job well done. As with the lesson book we recommend that the teacher remove the sticker sheet as the student begins each book. This preserves the element of surprise and increases motivation.

Consideration of the **Music Maker** reward stickers for each exercise is ideally withheld until the student has first mastered the basic elements of the music in question such as key signature, time signature, notes and rhythm.

Each **Finger Gym** page corresponds directly with the material covered in **Beanstalk's Basics for Piano Lesson Books** and works to further reinforce the technical challenges introduced.

Finger Gym contains another motivational tool known as '**Coach's Corner**.' Here the student is challenged to perform and record several repetitions of each exercise. We encourage students to perform their 'repetitions' five days each week with the remaining two days left to parents' and teachers' discretion.

We wish much success and enjoyment to all **Finger Gym** participants!

To
Alanna & Brianne

CHERYL FINN   **EAMONN MORRIS**

COACH'S CORNER
Do 5 repetitions each day.
1 2 3 4 5 (6) (7)
Day: ✓

TECH TIP

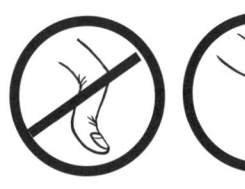

Be sure that your fingers are **CURVED** when you play and that you play with **STRONG FINGERTIPS**!

MUSIC MAKER
1. Curved fingers and strong fingertips.

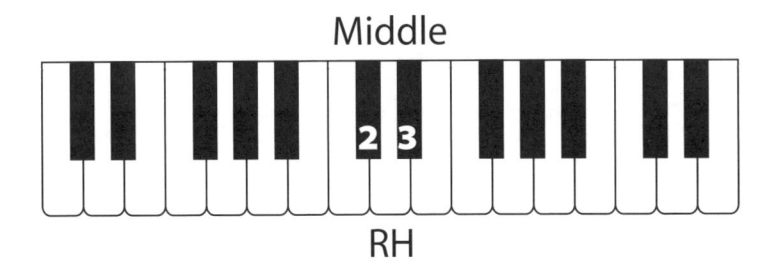

WIGGLE WARM-UP RIGHT!

RH 2 3 2 3 | 2 3 2 3 |

2 3 2 3 | 2 3 2 2 ||

Continue playing on each group of two black keys all the way up to the top of the keyboard!

CORRESPONDS WITH PAGE 7 OF BEANSTALK'S LESSON BOOK PREP A.

COACH'S CORNER
Do 5 repetitions each day.

Day:	1	2	3	4	5	(6)	(7)
	✓						

TECH TIP

Be sure that your fingers are **CURVED** when you play and that you play with **STRONG FINGERTIPS**!

MUSIC MAKER
2. Curved fingers and strong fingertips.

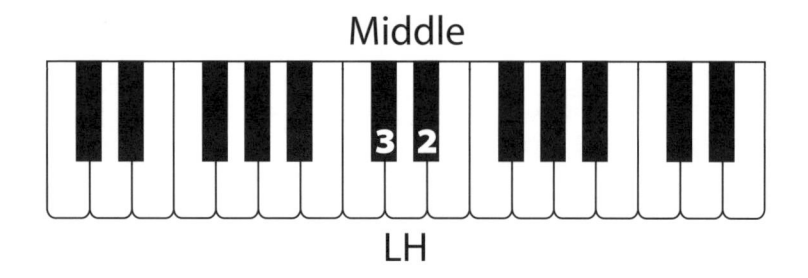

Middle

3 2

LH

WIGGLE WARM-UP LEFT!

LH

3 2 3 2 3 2 3 2

3 2 3 2 3 2 3 3

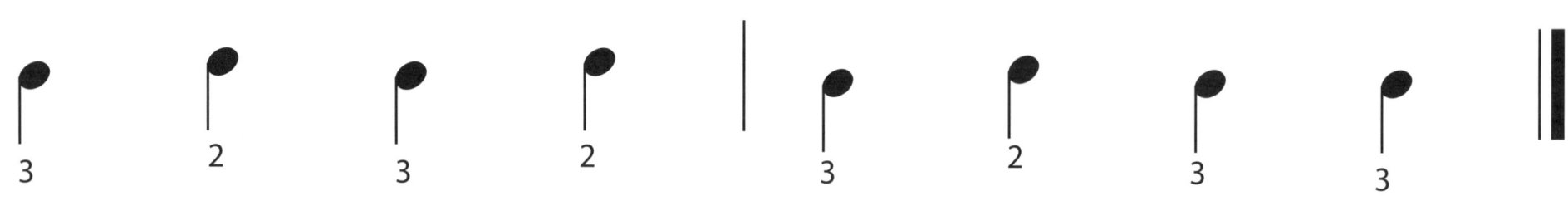

Continue playing on each group of two black keys all the way down to the bottom of the keyboard!

CORRESPONDS WITH PAGE 8 OF BEANSTALK'S LESSON BOOK PREP A.

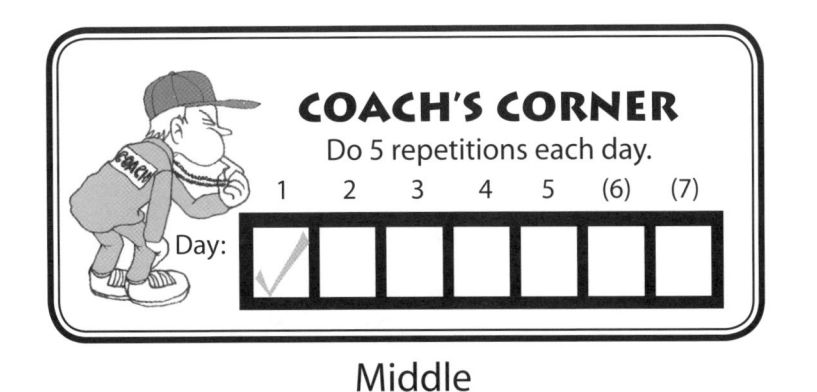

COACH'S CORNER
Do 5 repetitions each day.

Day:	1	2	3	4	5	(6)	(7)
	✓						

MUSIC MAKER

3. Curved fingers and strong fingertips.

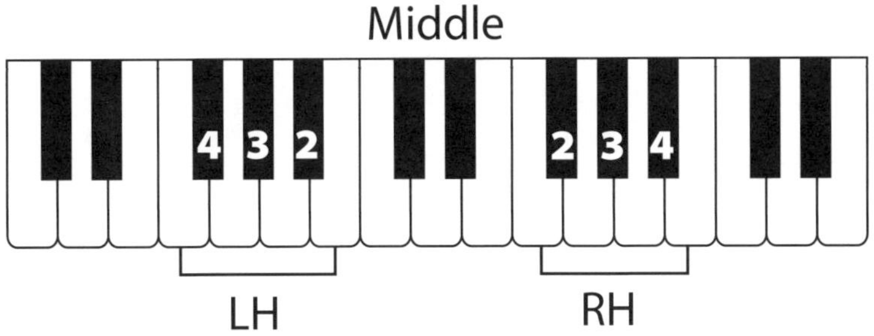

Middle

LH RH

WEIGHT LIFTING

RH: 4 3 | 4 3 4 3 | 4 3 | 4 3 4

LH: 4 3 | 4 3 4 3 4 | 3 | 4 3 4

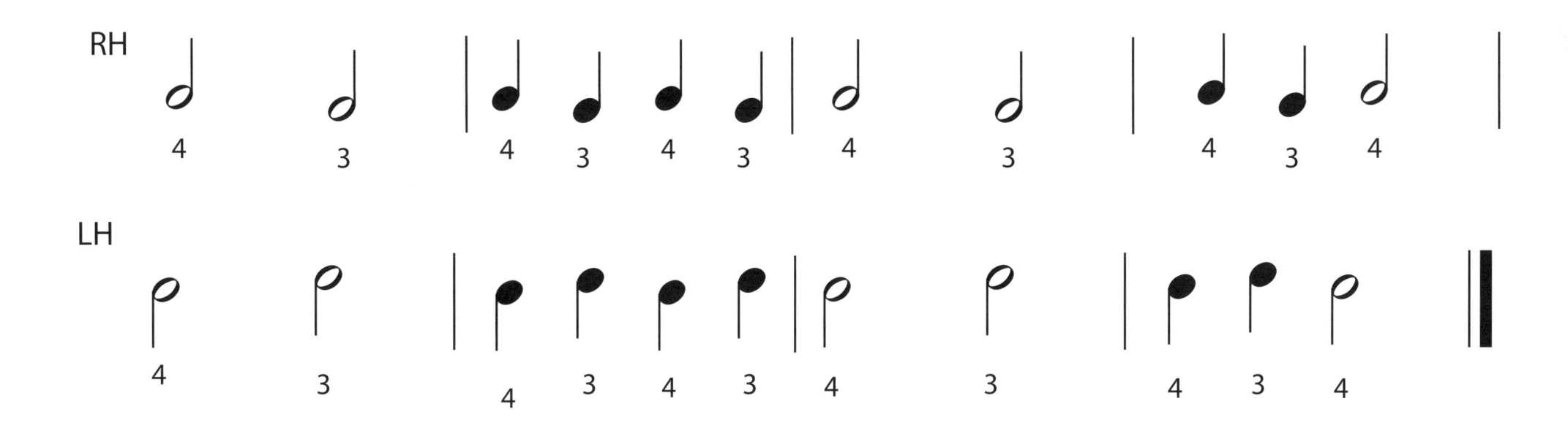

CORRESPONDS WITH PAGES 9 & 10 OF BEANSTALK'S LESSON BOOK PREP A.

COACH'S CORNER
Do 5 repetitions each day.

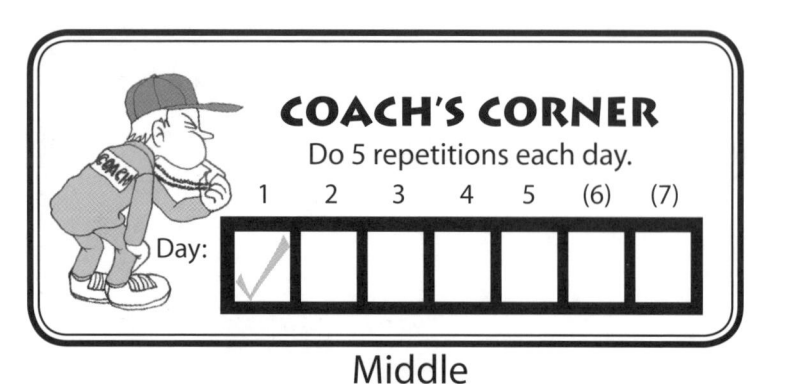

| 1 | 2 | 3 | 4 | 5 | (6) | (7) |

Day: ✓

MUSIC MAKER
4. Curved fingers and strong fingertips.

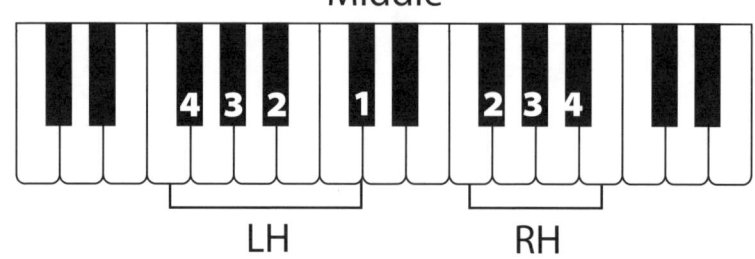

BICYCLE RACE

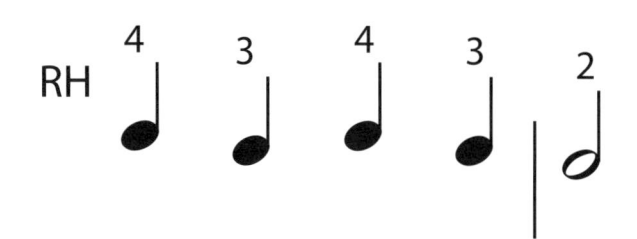

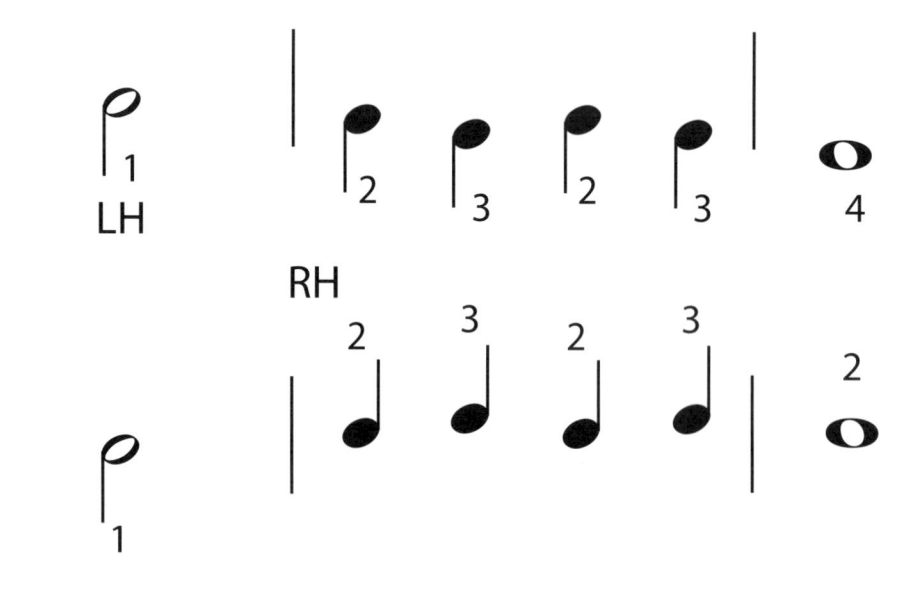

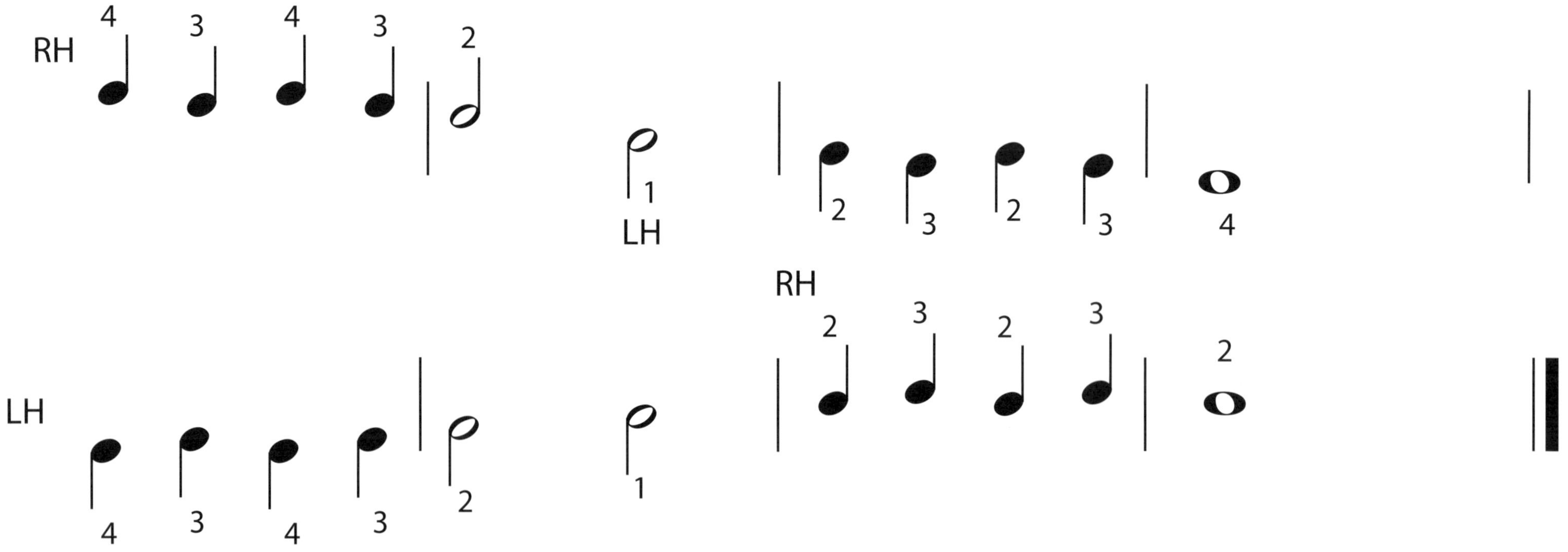

CORRESPONDS WITH PAGES 11 & 12 OF BEANSTALK'S LESSON BOOK PREP A.

COACH'S CORNER

Do 5 repetitions each day.

1	2	3	4	5	(6)	(7)

Day: ✓

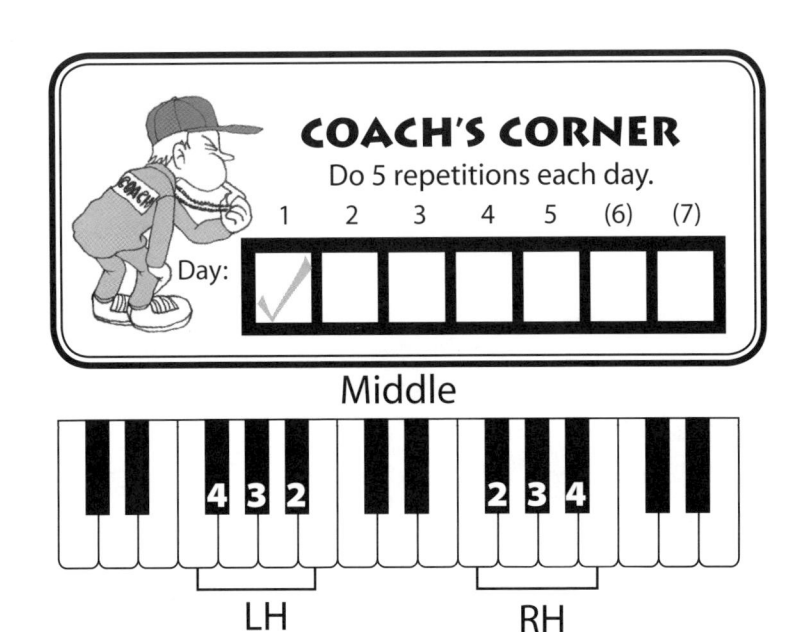

Middle

LH 4 3 2   RH 2 3 4

TECH TIP

To play **LOUDLY**, make your arms feel heavy.

IMAGINE

you have a weight placed on your forearm.

MUSIC MAKER

5. Play loudly using strong fingertips.

DOING FREE WEIGHTS

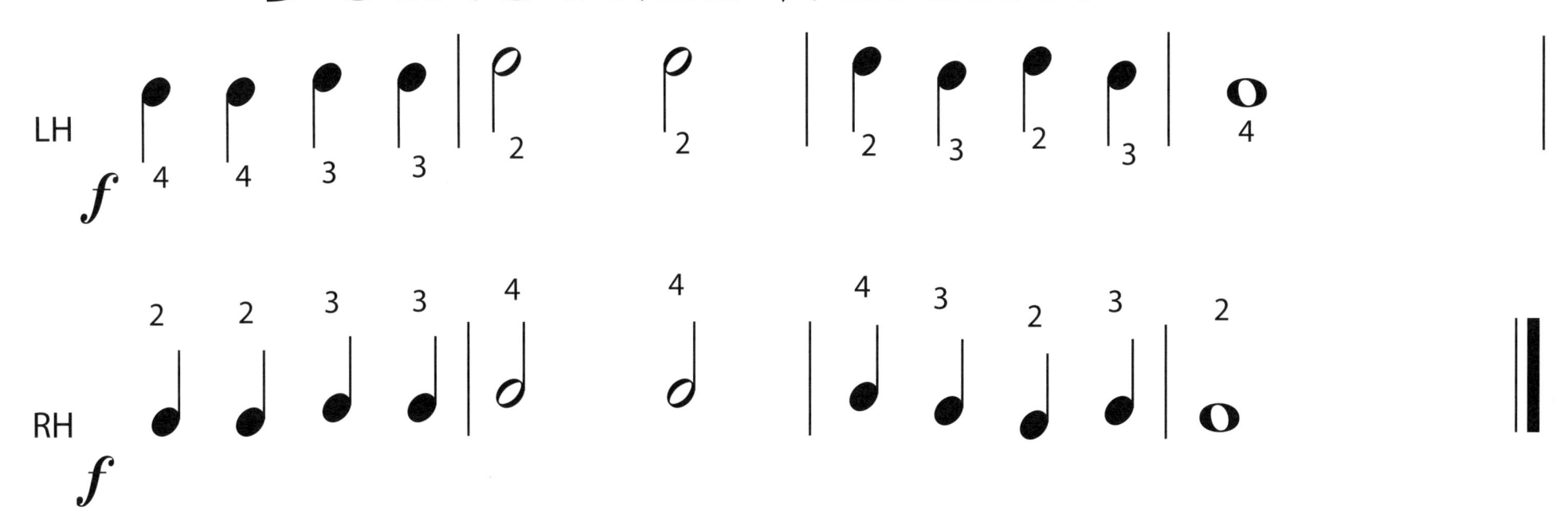

LH *f* 4 4 3 3 2 2 2 3 2 3 4

RH 2 2 3 3 4 4 4 3 2 3 2 *f*

CORRESPONDS WITH PAGE 13 OF BEANSTALK'S LESSON BOOK PREP A.

COACH'S CORNER
Do 5 repetitions each day.

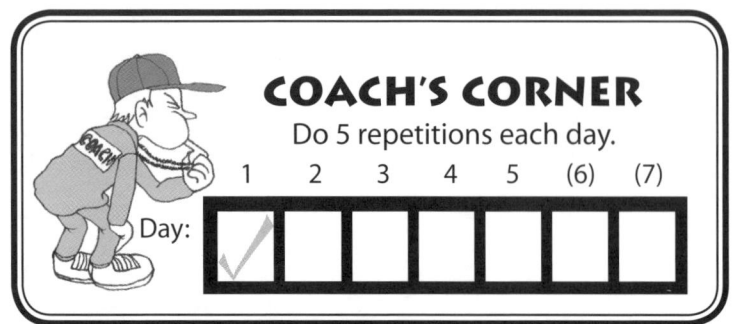

| Day: | 1 ✓ | 2 | 3 | 4 | 5 | (6) | (7) |

TECH TIP
To play **SOFTLY** make your arms feel light.

IMAGINE
your fingers are tippytoeing across the keys.

MUSIC MAKER
6. Play softly using strong fingertips.

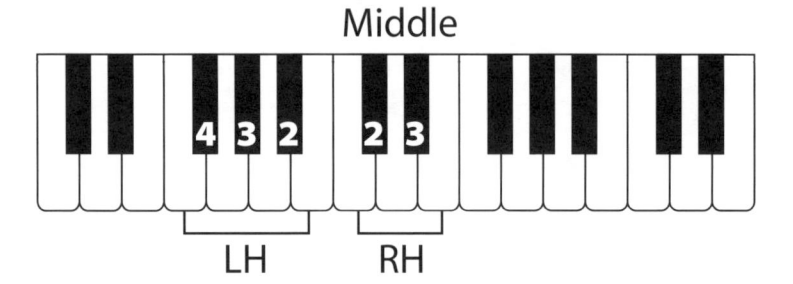

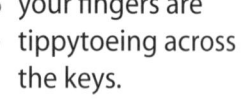

WALKING ON TIPPYTOES

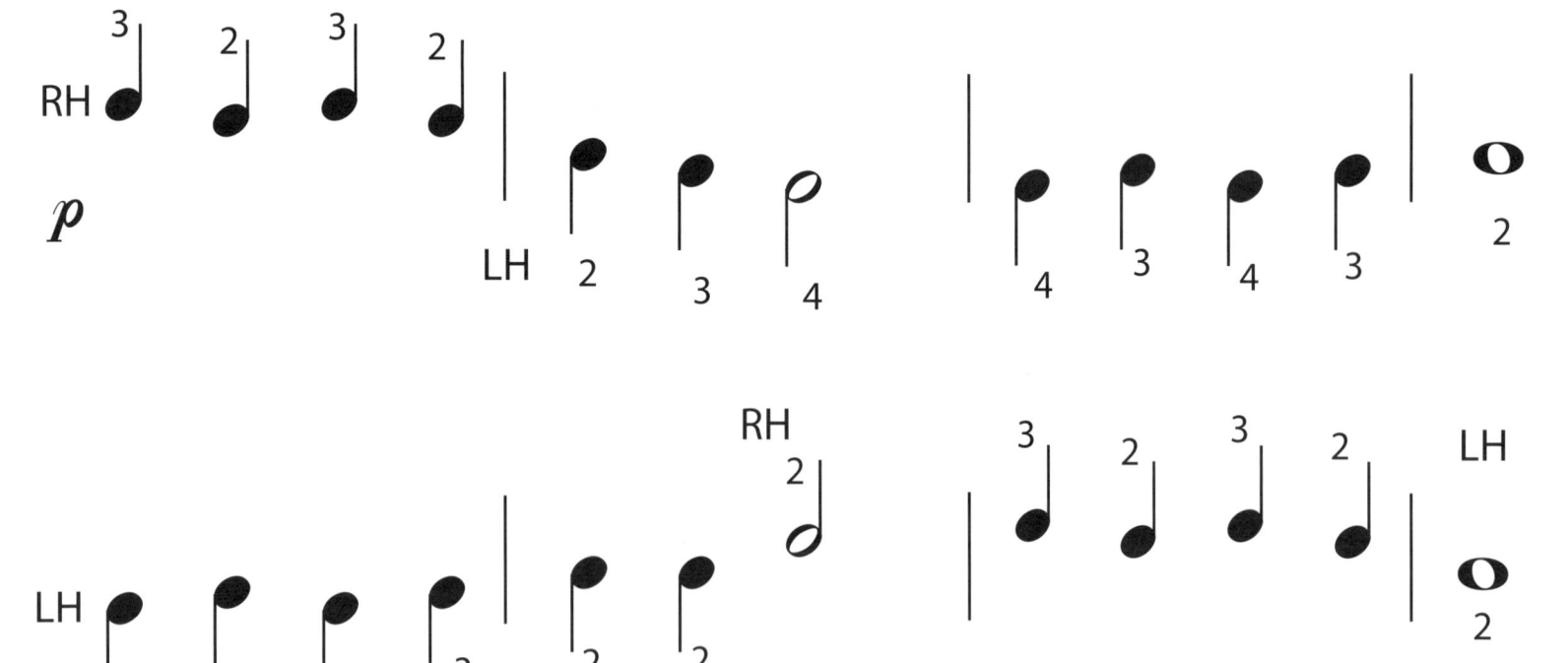

CORRESPONDS WITH PAGE 14 OF BEANSTALK'S LESSON BOOK PREP A.

COACH'S CORNER
Do 5 repetitions each day.

Day:	1	2	3	4	5	(6)	(7)
✓							

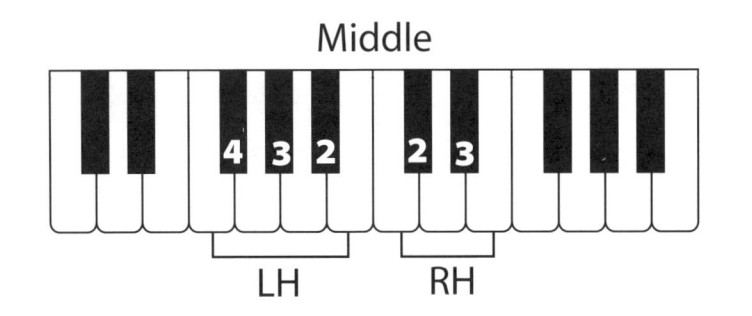

Middle — LH 4 3 2 / RH 2 3

MUSIC MAKER
7. Play loudly and softly using strong fingertips.

PLAYING COPY CAT!

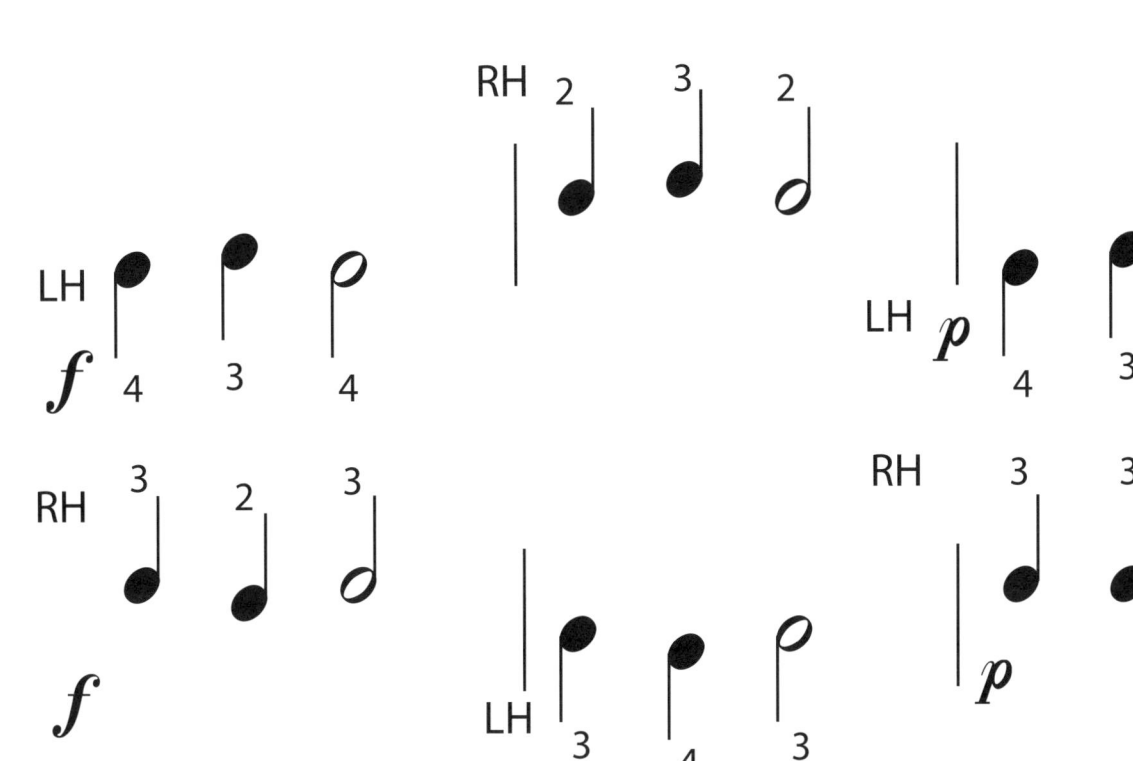

CORRESPONDS WITH PAGE 15 OF BEANSTALK'S LESSON BOOK PREP A.

COACH'S CORNER

Do 5 repetitions each day.

Day:	1	2	3	4	5	(6)	(7)
	✓						

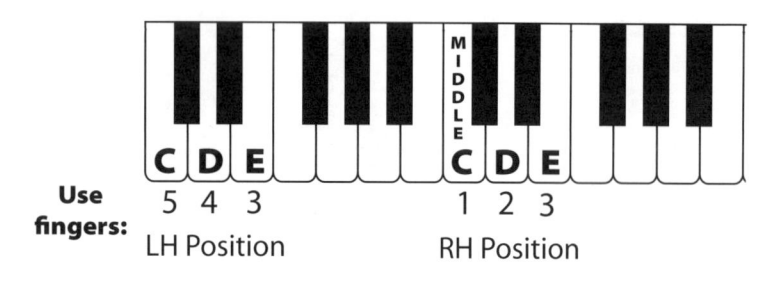

Use fingers:

LH Position: C D E — 5 4 3
RH Position: Middle C D E — 1 2 3

MUSIC MAKER

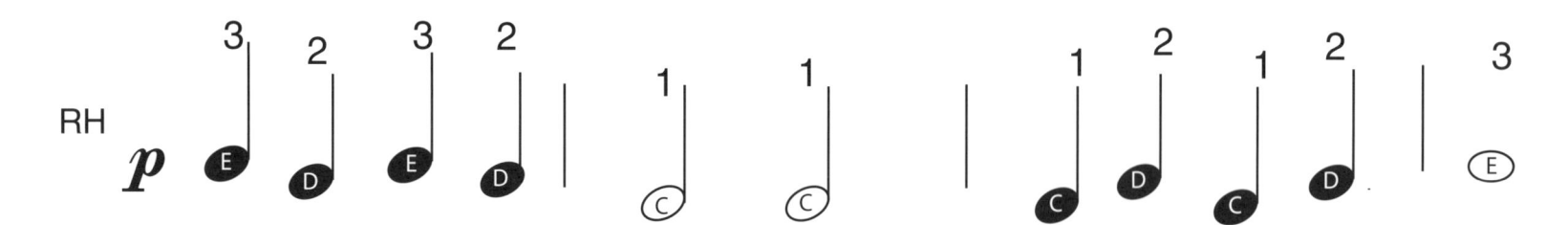

8. Play loudly and softly using strong fingertips.

SPINNING AROUND!

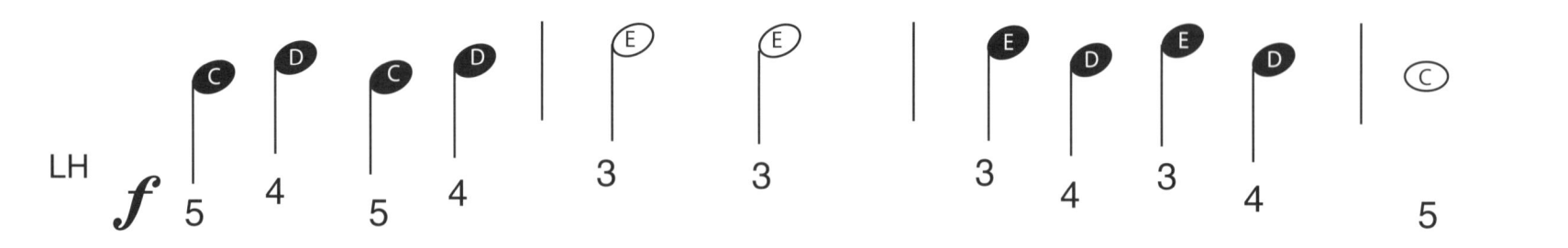

RH: *p* — E(3) D(2) E(3) D(2) | C(1) C(1) | C(1) D(2) C(1) D(2) | E(3)

LH: *f* — C(5) D(4) C(5) D(4) | E(3) E(3) | E(3) D(4) E(3) D(4) | C(5)

CORRESPONDS WITH PAGE 18 OF BEANSTALK'S LESSON BOOK PREP A.

COACH'S CORNER
Do 5 repetitions each day.

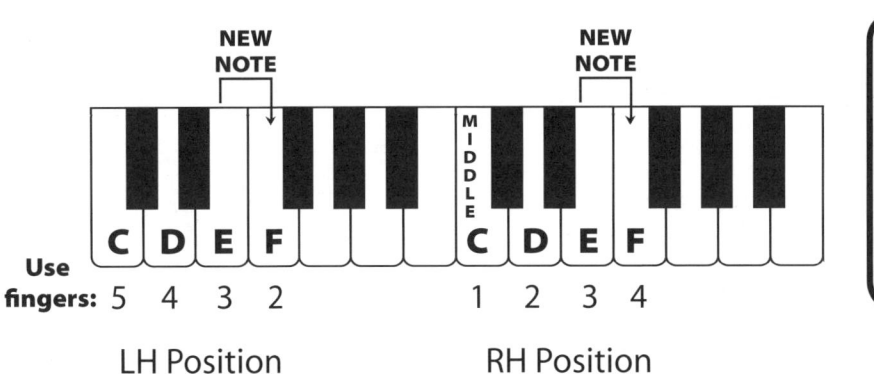

Day: 1 ✓ 2 3 4 5 (6) (7)

MUSIC MAKER
9. Play loudly and softly using strong fingertips.

NEW NOTE — LH Position: C D E F, Use fingers: 5 4 3 2

NEW NOTE — RH Position (Middle C): C D E F, fingers: 1 2 3 4

HIGH STEPPING

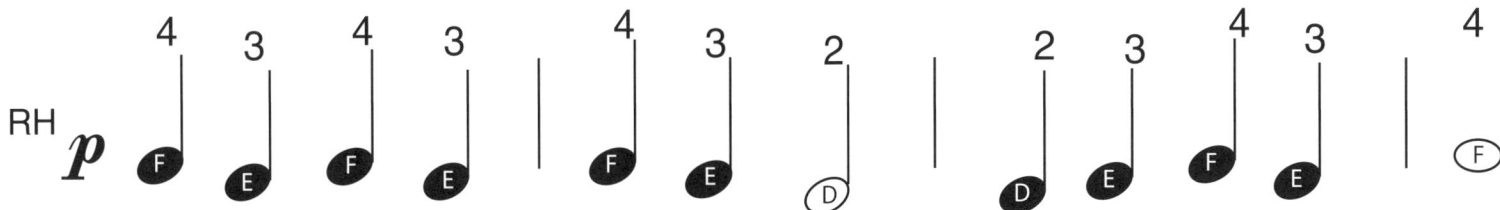

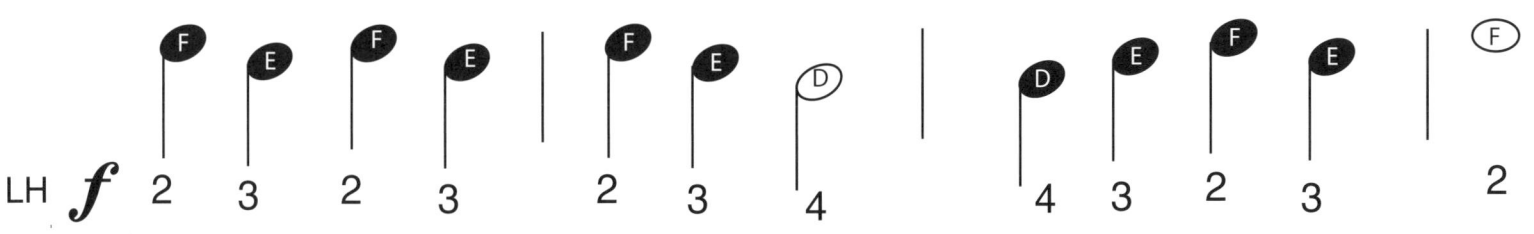

RH p — F(4) E(3) F(4) E(3) | F(4) E(3) D(2) | D(2) E(3) F(4) E(3) | F(4)

LH f — F(2) E(3) F(2) E(3) | F(2) E(3) D(4) | D(4) E(3) F(2) E(3) | F(2)

CORRESPONDS WITH PAGE 19 OF BEANSTALK'S LESSON BOOK PREP A.

COACH'S CORNER

Do 5 repetitions each day.

Day:	1	2	3	4	5	(6)	(7)
	✓						

NEW C POSITION NEW
NOTE / NOTE

Use fingers: 5 4 3 2 1 | 1 2 3 4 5

LH Position — RH Position

MUSIC MAKER

10. Play loudly and softly using strong fingertips.

WHEEL BARROW RACE!

RH: G F E D | C D E F | G F E D | E | E
f

LH: C D E F | G F E D | C D E D | C | C
p

CORRESPONDS WITH PAGE 20 OF BEANSTALK'S LESSON BOOK PREP A.

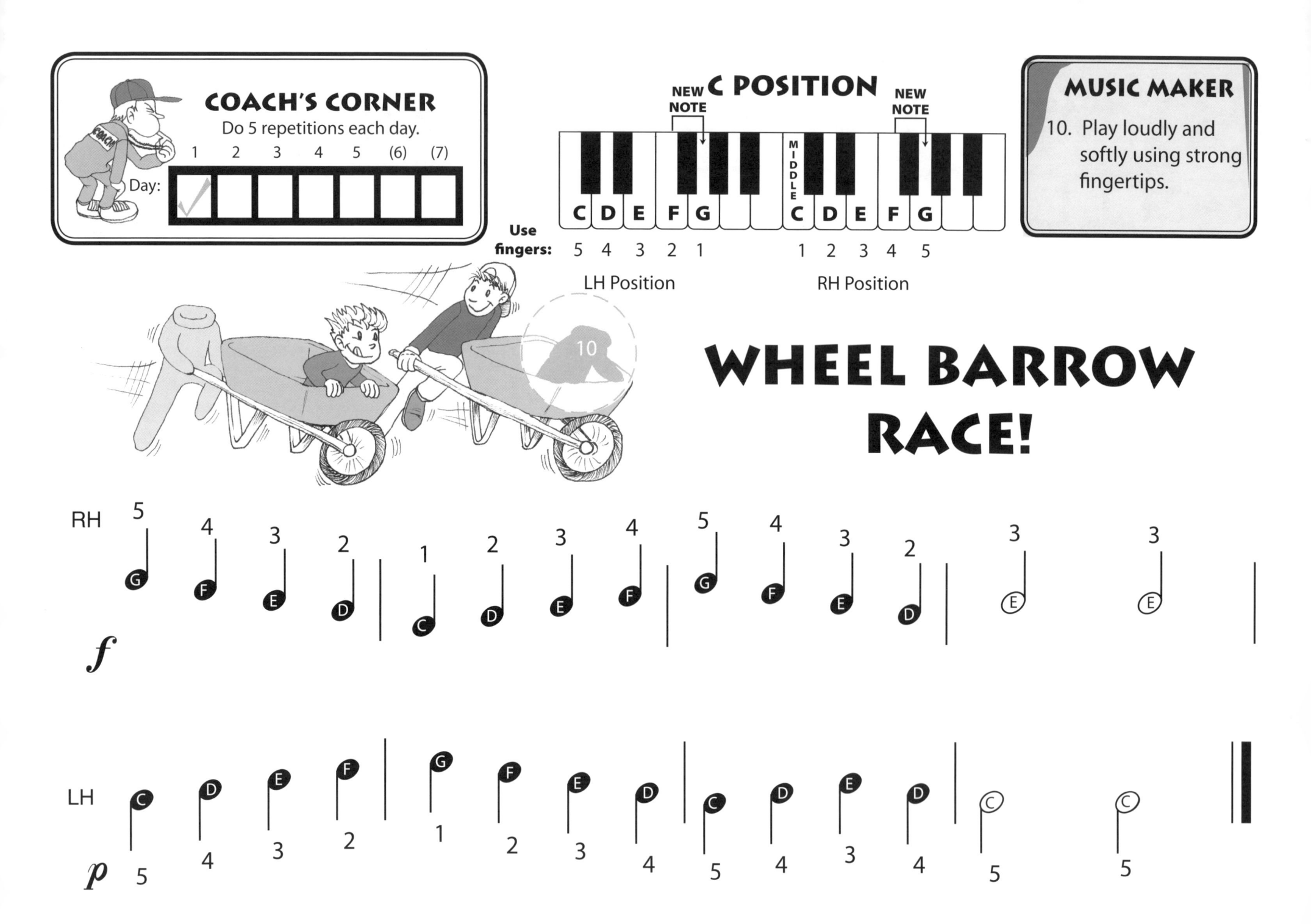

COACH'S CORNER

Do 5 repetitions each day.

Day:	1	2	3	4	5	(6)	(7)
	✓						

TECH TIP

To play **SMOOTHLY**, hold down each key and lift only when you are about to play the next key.

MUSIC MAKER

11. Play smoothly.

C POSITION

C D E F G C D E F G

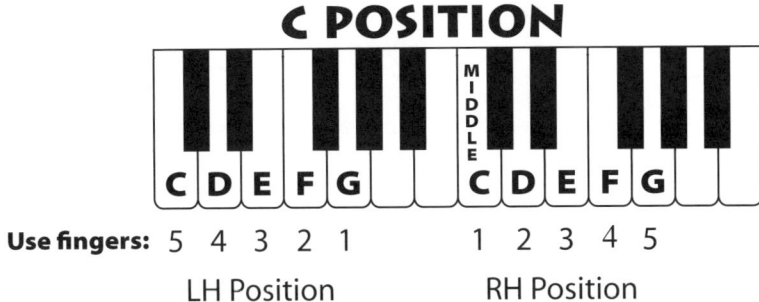

Use fingers: 5 4 3 2 1   1 2 3 4 5

LH Position   RH Position

IMAGINE

your fingers are go-ing for a walk!

WALKING FINGERS

LH
$\frac{4}{4}$ G F E D C D E F G F E D C
f 1

RH
1 C D E F G F E D C D E D C
p

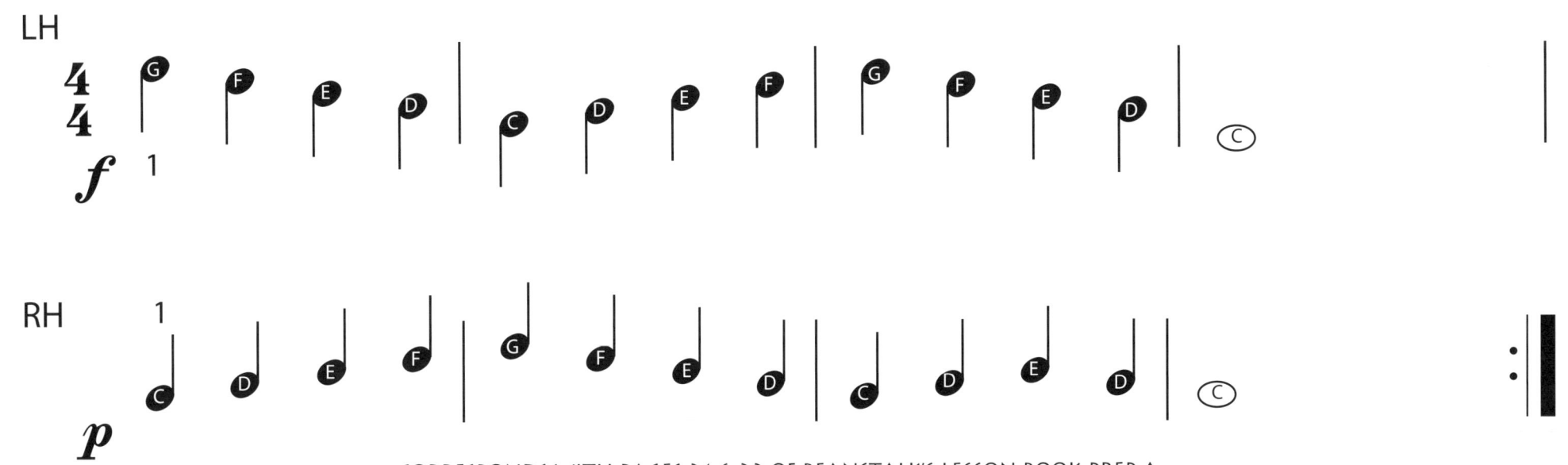

CORRESPONDS WITH PAGES 21 & 22 OF BEANSTALK'S LESSON BOOK PREP A.

COACH'S CORNER

Do 5 repetitions each day.

Day:	1	2	3	4	5	(6)	(7)
	✓						

MUSIC MAKER

12. Play smoothly.

FINGER MARCH

CORRESPONDS WITH PAGES 23 & 24 OF BEANSTALK'S LESSON BOOK PREP A.

COACH'S CORNER
Do 5 repetitions each day.

Day:	1	2	3	4	5	(6)	(7)
	✓						

MUSIC MAKER
13. Play smoothly.

STRETCHING

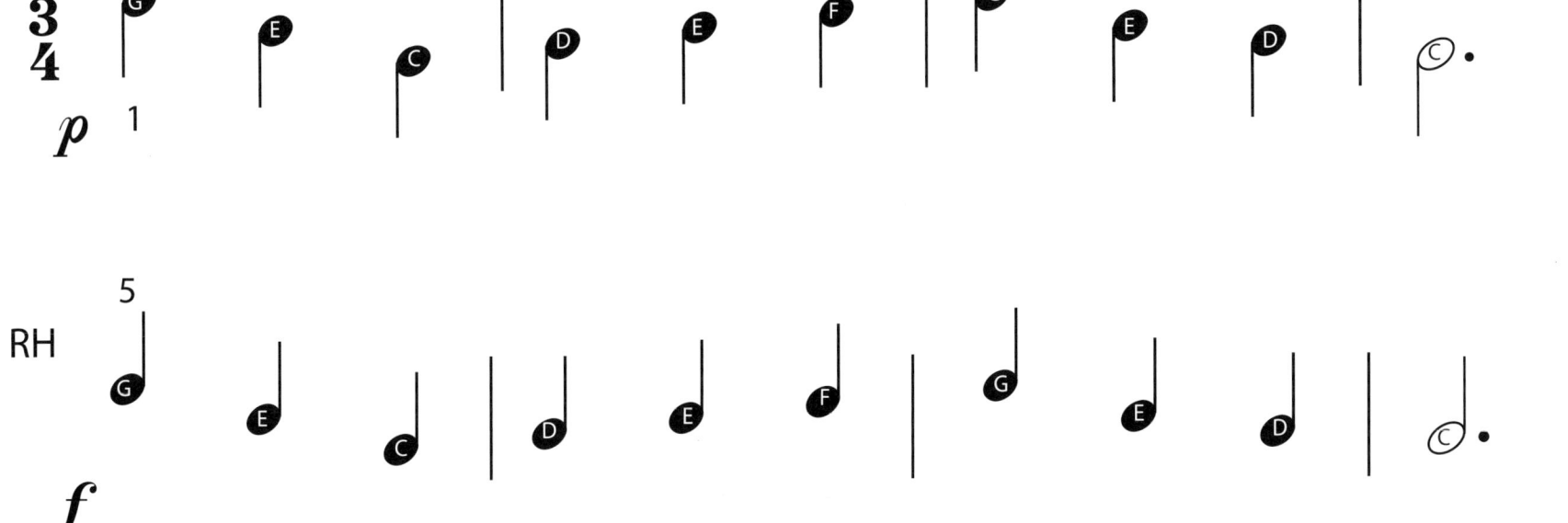

CORRESPONDS WITH PAGES 25 & 26 OF BEANSTALK'S LESSON BOOK PREP A.

COACH'S CORNER
Do 5 repetitions each day.

Day:	1	2	3	4	5	(6)	(7)
	✓						

TECH TIP! Hand position is very important when you play. In a good hand position your thumb should **STAND UP** and be **STRONG**. (It should not lie flat or curl up.)

MUSIC MAKER
14. Strong thumb.

Use fingers: 1 2 3

SOCCER TRY-OUTS!

Steadily

f

Continue repeating this exercise starting on each C all the way to the top.

Count: 1 - 2 - 3 - 4

ARM SWINGS
To add finesse and musicality to your playing, try adding **ARM SWINGS**. In this series, arm swings are marked with arrows ( ) showing the direction of the swing (Swing arm out **RIGHT** : Swing arm out **LEFT** :). **SLOWLY** and **GENTLY** move your arm out, away from your sides for the value of the given note. Then **GRACEFULLY** lift off the key. It's like drawing a happy face with your elbow.
Here are some ARM SWING warm-ups for you to try with your right hand.

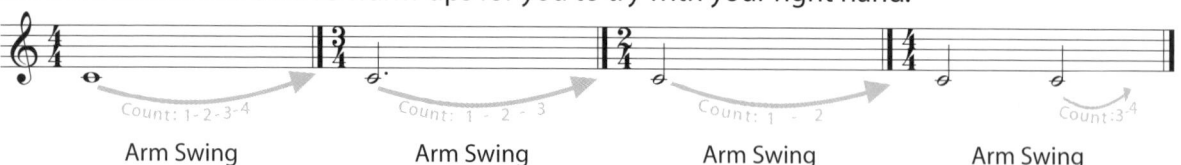

Count: 1-2-3-4   Count: 1-2-3   Count: 1-2   Count: 3-4

Arm Swing   Arm Swing   Arm Swing   Arm Swing

CORRESPONDS WITH PAGE 28 OF BEANSTALK'S LESSON BOOK PREP A.

COACH'S CORNER
Do 5 repetitions each day.

| Day: | 1 | 2 | 3 | 4 | 5 | (6) | (7) |

MUSIC MAKER
15. Strong thumb.

SOCCER GAME WARM-UPS

HOME TEAM

Steadily

f

Arm Swing Count: 3 - 4

VISITING TEAM

Steadily

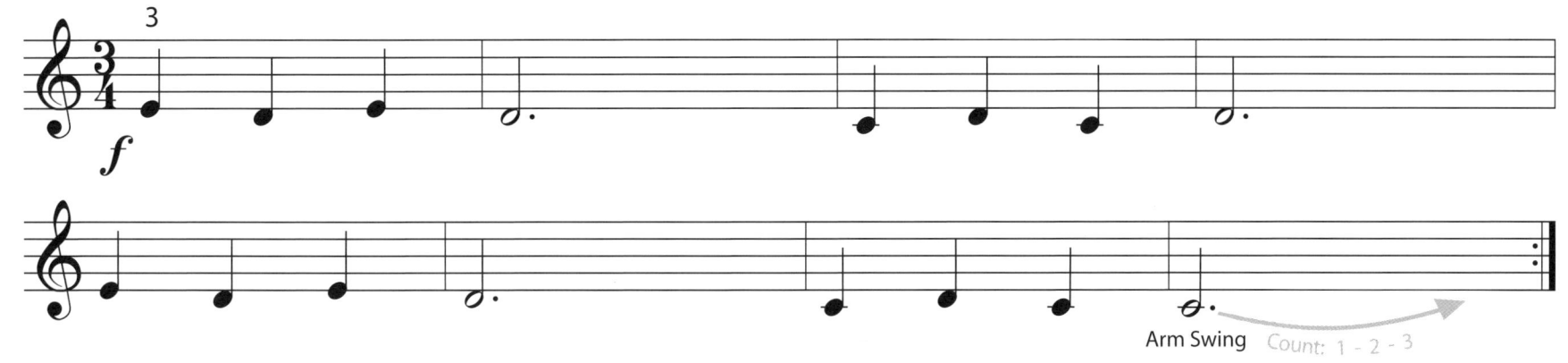

f

Arm Swing Count: 1 - 2 - 3

CORRESPONDS WITH PAGE 29 OF BEANSTALK'S LESSON BOOK PREP A.

COACH'S CORNER
Do 5 repetitions each day.

Day:	1	2	3	4	5	(6)	(7)

TECH TIP! In a good hand position, your 5th finger tip should **STAND UP** and be **STRONG**. (It should not lie flat or roll over).

MUSIC MAKER

16. Strong 5th finger.

LH POSITION

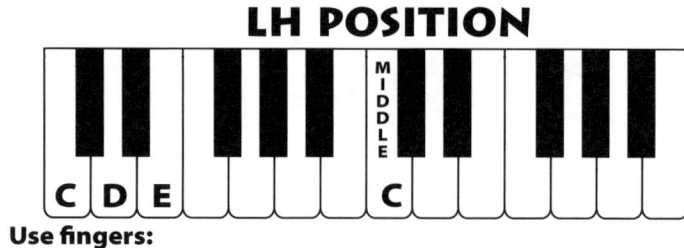

C D E — MIDDLE C

Use fingers: 5 4 3

BASEBALL TRY-OUTS!

Steadily

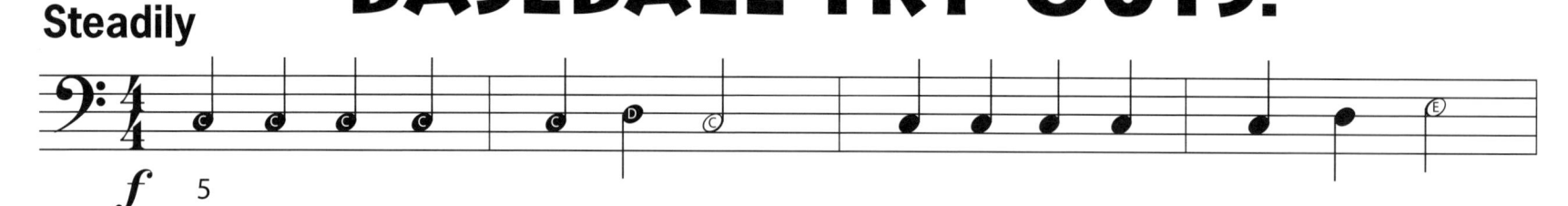

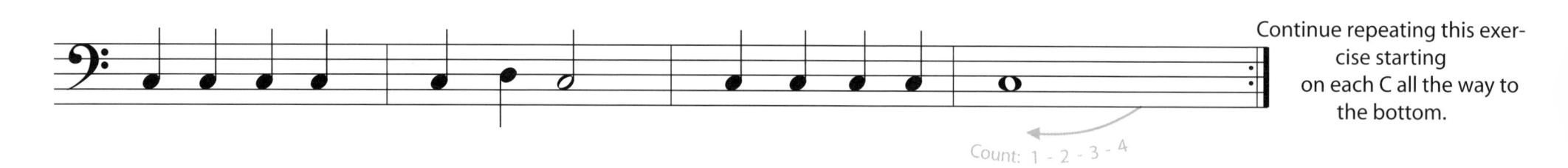

f 5

Continue repeating this exercise starting on each C all the way to the bottom.

Count: 1 - 2 - 3 - 4

Here are some **ARM SWING** warm-ups for you to try with your left hand.

Count: 1-2-3-4
Arm Swing

Count: 1-2-3
Arm Swing

Count: 1-2
Arm Swing

Count: 3-4
Arm Swing

CORRESPONDS WITH PAGE 30 OF BEANSTALK'S LESSON BOOK PREP A.

18 12461

COACH'S CORNER
Do 5 repetitions each day.

Day:	1	2	3	4	5	(6)	(7)
	✓						

MUSIC MAKER
17. Strong 5th finger.

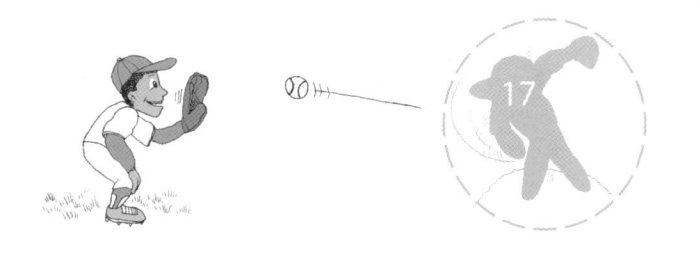

BASEBALL GAME WARM-UPS

HOME TEAM

Steadily

Count: 3-4
Arm Swing

VISITING TEAM

Steadily

Count: 1-2
Arm Swing

CORRESPONDS WITH PAGE 31 OF BEANSTALK'S LESSON BOOK PREP A.

COACH'S CORNER
Do 5 repetitions each day.

RIGHT HAND C POSITION

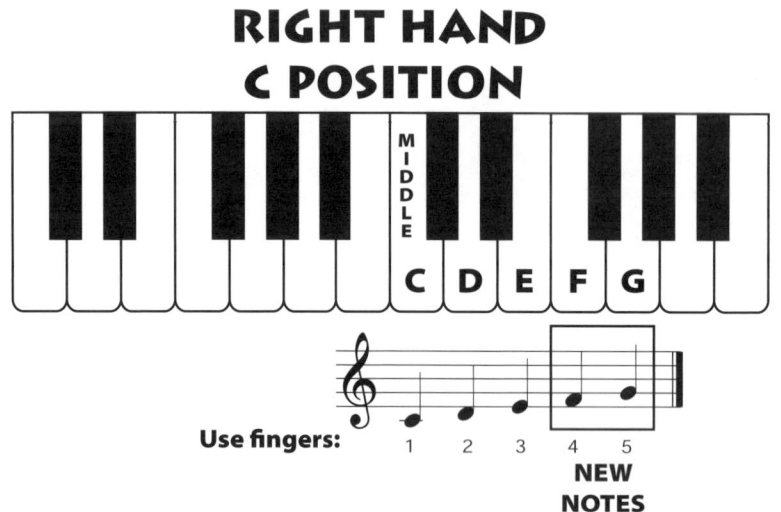

C D E F G

Use fingers: 1 2 3 4 5
NEW NOTES

MUSIC MAKER
18. Strong 5th finger.

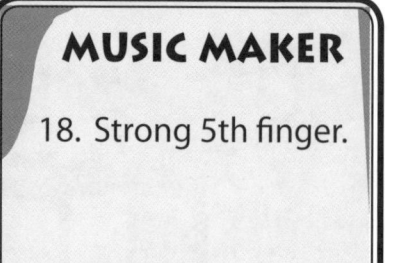

VOLLEYBALL TRY-OUTS!

Steadily

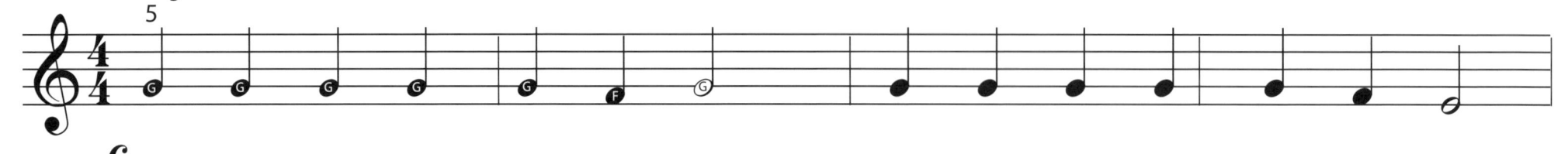

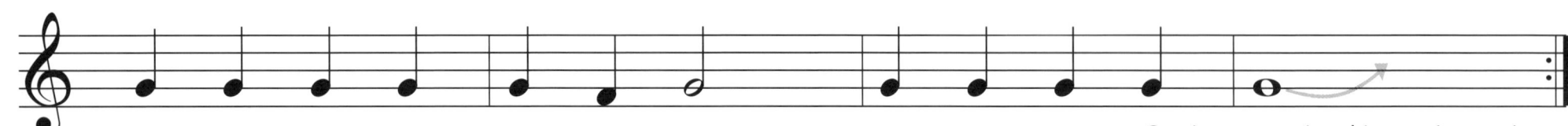

f

Continue repeating this exercise starting on each G all the way to the top.

CORRESPONDS WITH PAGE 32 OF BEANSTALK'S LESSON BOOK PREP A.

COACH'S CORNER
Do 5 repetitions each day.

1	2	3	4	5	(6)	(7)
✓						

Day:

MUSIC MAKER
19. Strong 5th finger.

VOLLEYBALL GAME WARM-UPS

Moderately

HOME TEAM

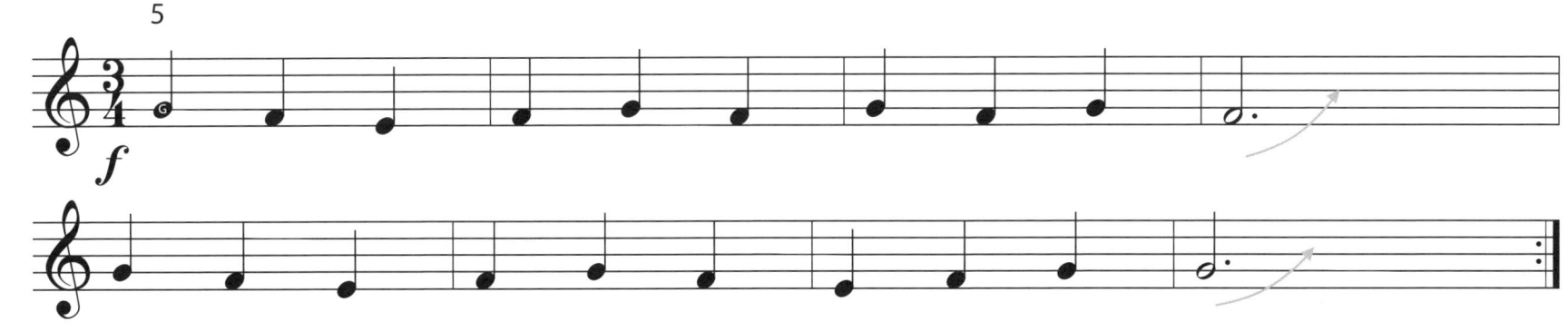

Moderately

VISITING TEAM

CORRESPONDS WITH PAGE 33 OF BEANSTALK'S LESSON BOOK PREP A.

COACH'S CORNER
Do 5 repetitions each day.

LEFT HAND C POSITION

MUSIC MAKER
20. Strong thumb.

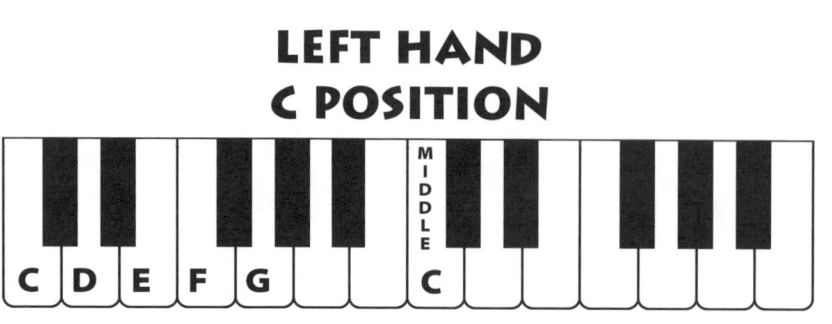

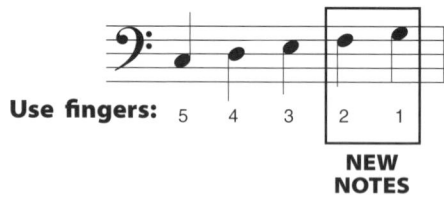

Use fingers: 5 4 3 2 1

NEW NOTES

SWIM TEAM TRY-OUTS!
Steadily

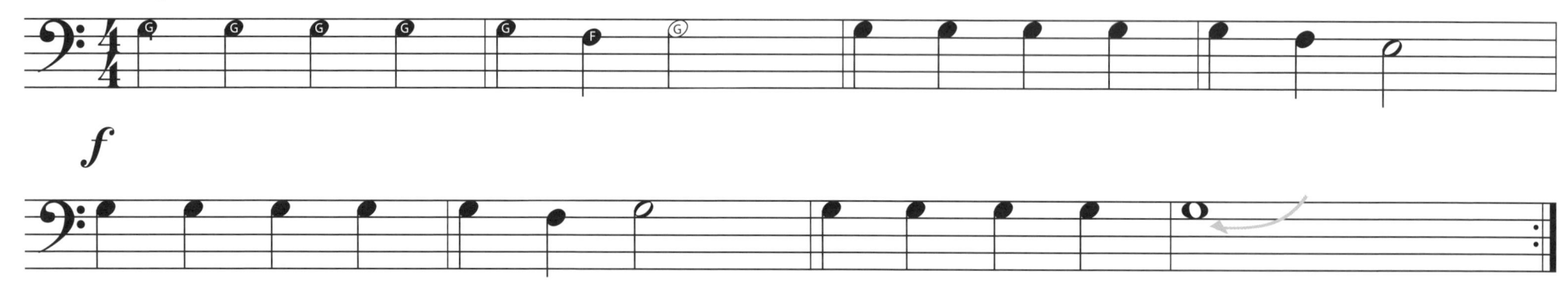

f

Continue repeating this exercise starting on each G all the way down to the bottom.

CORRESPONDS WITH PAGE 34 OF BEANSTALK'S LESSON BOOK PREP A.

COACH'S CORNER
Do 5 repetitions each day.

MUSIC MAKER

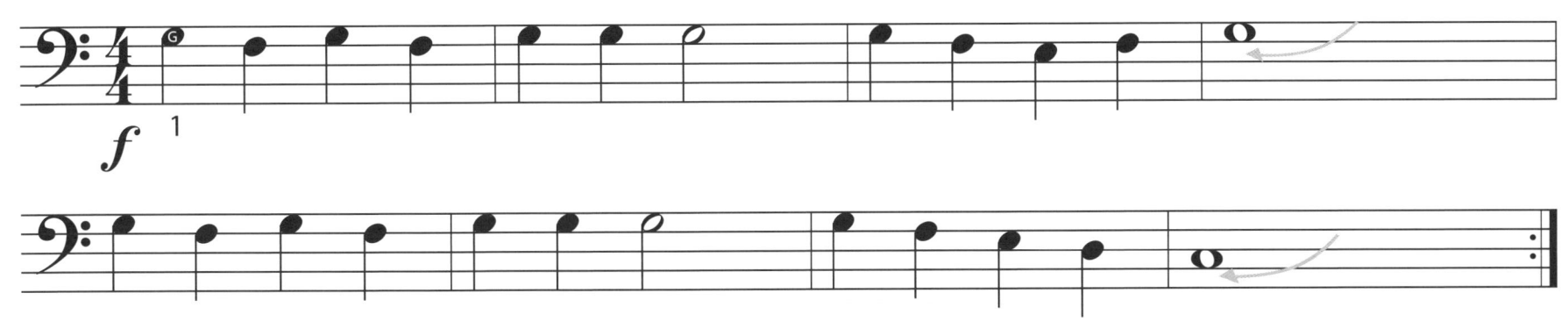

21. Strong thumb.

AT THE SWIM MEET!

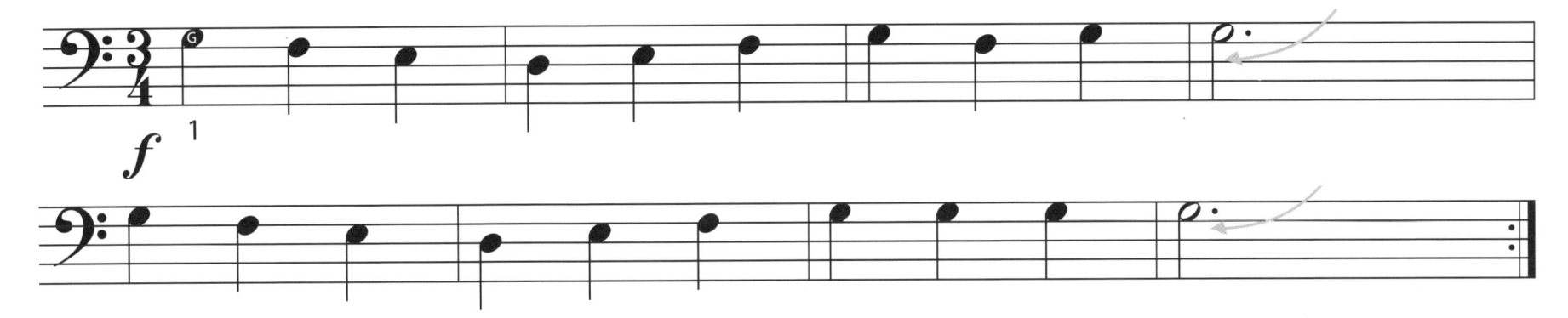

LANE 1
Moderately

LANE 2
Moderately

CORRESPONDS WITH PAGE 35 OF BEANSTALK'S LESSON BOOK PREP A.

COACH'S CORNER
Do 5 repetitions each day.

1	2	3	4	5	(6)	(7)

Day: ✓

C POSITION

MUSIC MAKER

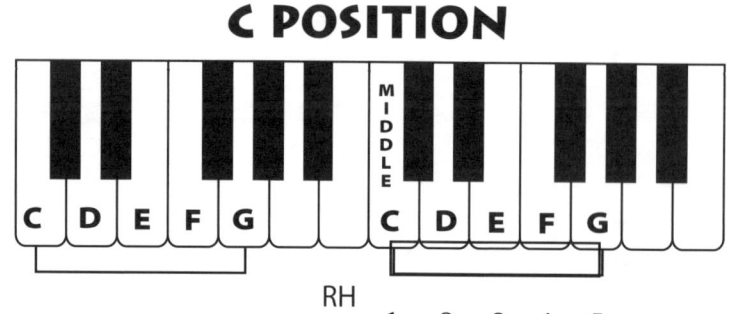

22. Strong thumb and 5th finger.

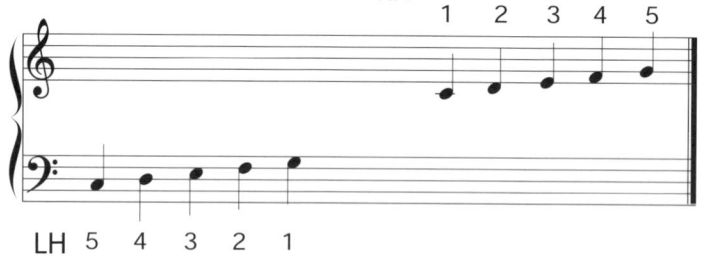

PLAYING FRISBEE

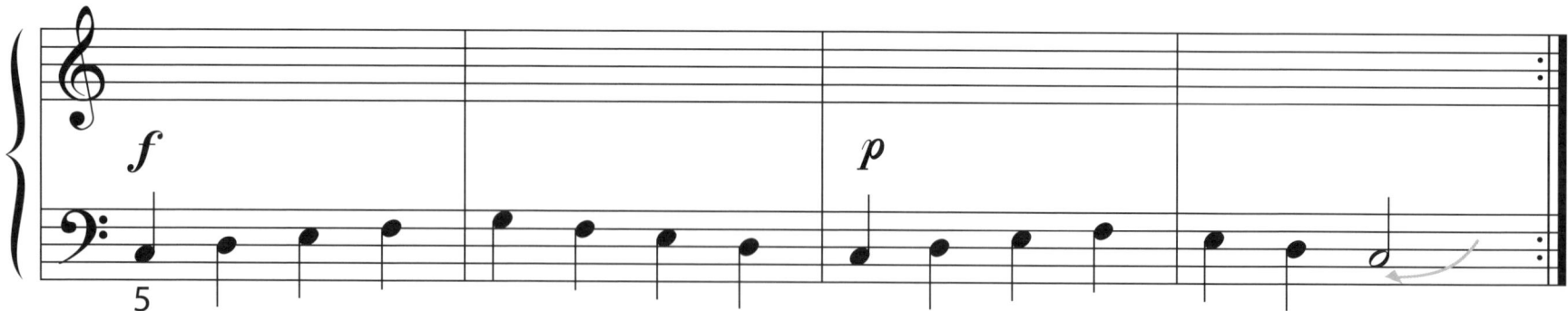

Steadily

CORRESPONDS WITH PAGE 37 OF BEANSTALK'S LESSON BOOK PREP A.

COACH'S CORNER
Do 5 repetitions each day.

MUSIC MAKER
23. Strong thumb and 5th finger.

ROPE CLIMBING

Steadily

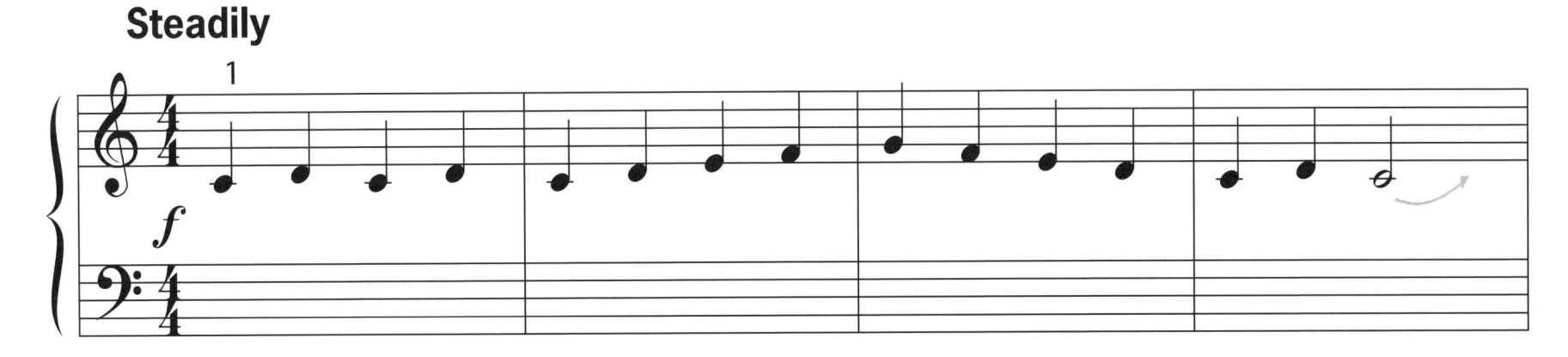

CORRESPONDS WITH PAGES 38 & 39 OF BEANSTALK'S LESSON BOOK PREP A.

COACH'S CORNER
Do 5 repetitions each day.

| Day: | 1 ✓ | 2 | 3 | 4 | 5 | (6) | (7) |

TECH TIP
An **EVEN TONE** ensures that your playing is **SMOOTH** and shows that you are in control. To develop an even tone, play each note in the passage with the same loudness—no bumps or weak notes!

MUSIC MAKER
24. Play smoothly with an even tone.

SOCCER DRILL

Smoothly

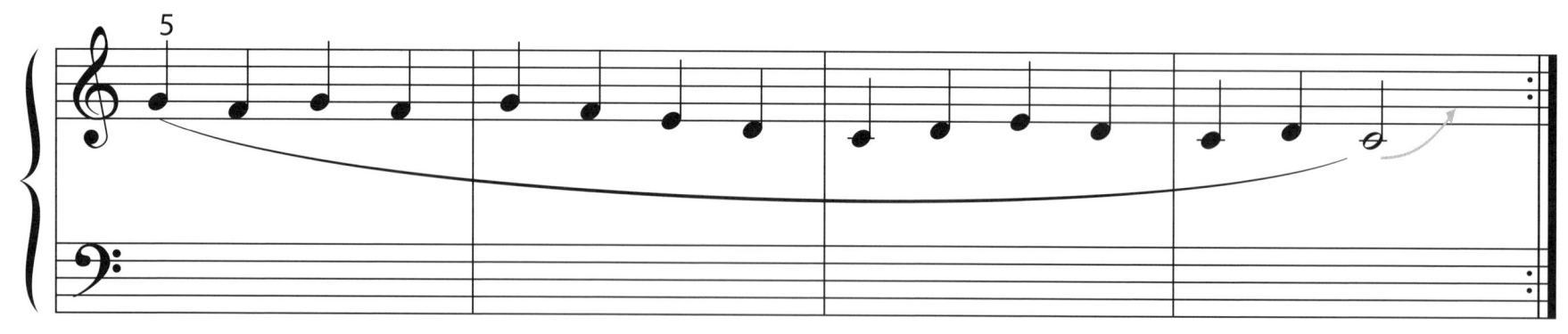

CORRESPONDS WITH PAGES 40 & 41 OF BEANSTALK'S LESSON BOOK PREP A.

COACH'S CORNER
Do 5 repetitions each day.

Day:	1	2	3	4	5	(6)	(7)
	✓						

MUSIC MAKER
25. Count steadily.

WALK AND REST!

Moderately

CORRESPONDS WITH PAGE 42 OF BEANSTALK'S LESSON BOOK PREP A.

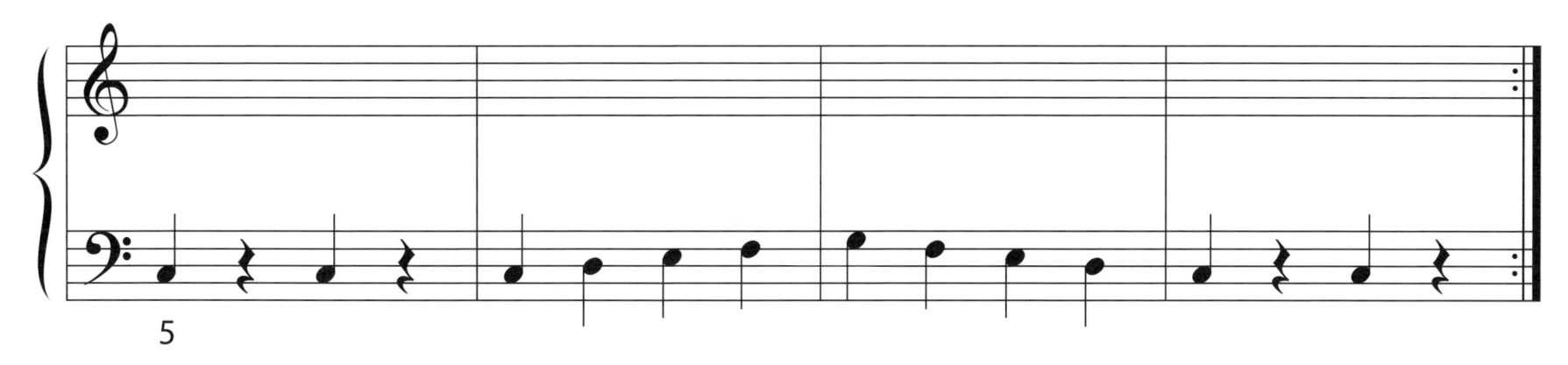

COACH'S CORNER
Do 5 repetitions each day.

MUSIC MAKER
26. Play smoothly with an even tone.

HOOLA HOOPS!

Steadily

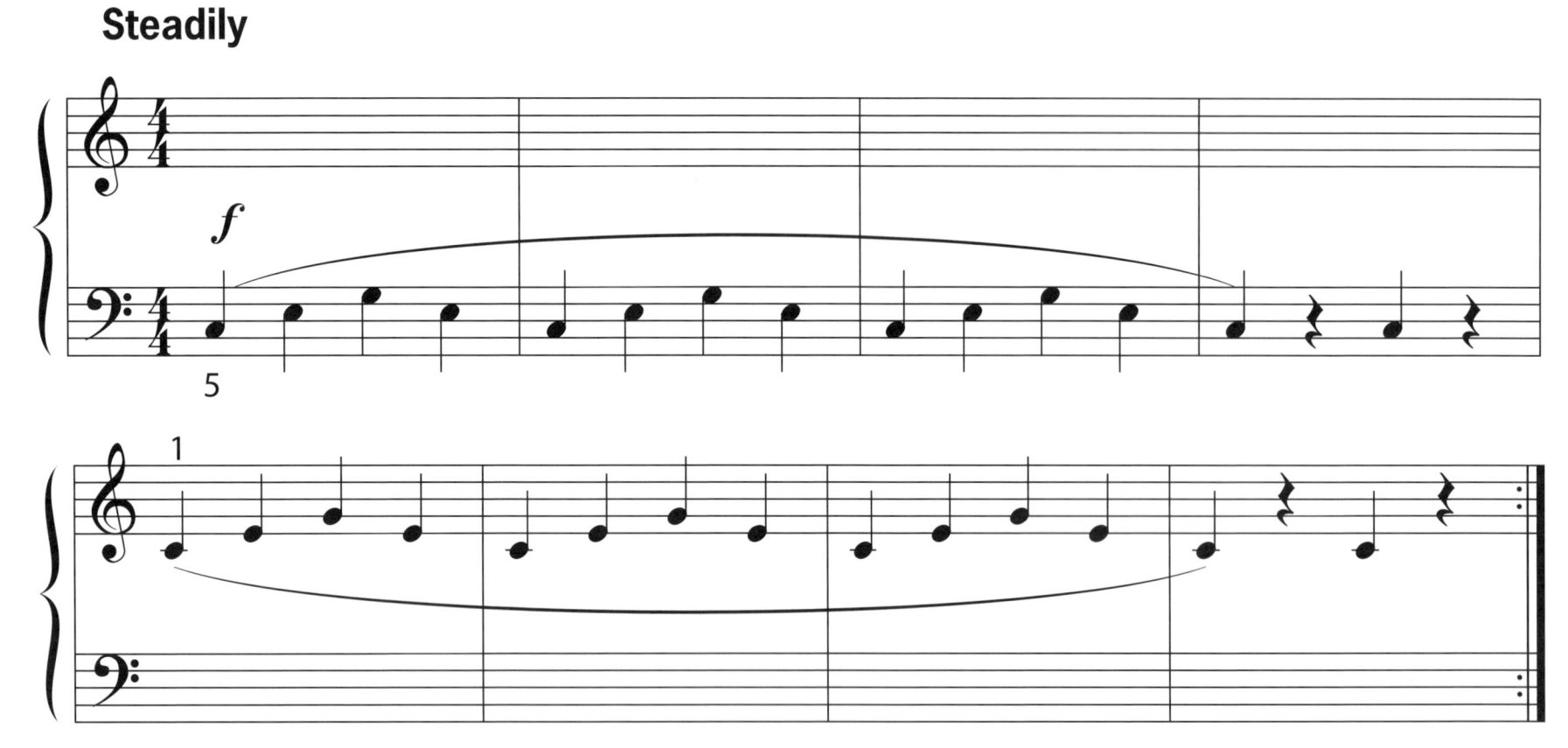

CORRESPONDS WITH PAGE 43 OF BEANSTALK'S LESSON BOOK PREP A.

COACH'S CORNER

Do 5 repetitions each day.

| 1 | 2 | 3 | 4 | 5 | (6) | (7) |

Day: ✓

MUSIC MAKER

27. Play smoothly with an even tone.

SKIPPING STONES

Smoothly

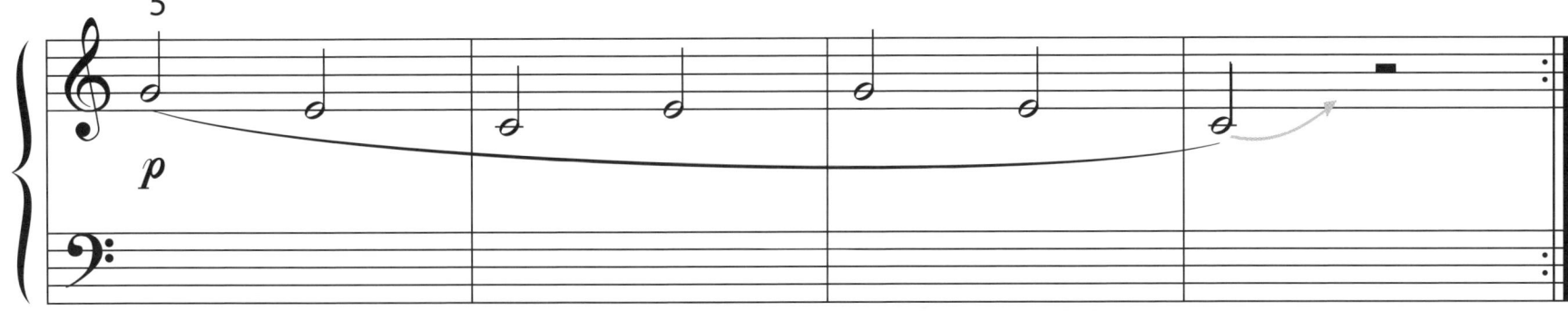

CORRESPONDS WITH PAGE 44 OF BEANSTALK'S LESSON BOOK PREP A.

COACH'S CORNER
Do 5 repetitions each day.

| 1 | 2 | 3 | 4 | 5 | (6) | (7) |

Day:

MUSIC MAKER
28. Play smoothly with an even tone.

TWIRLING AROUND

Smoothly

CORRESPONDS WITH PAGE 45 OF BEANSTALK'S LESSON BOOK PREP A.

COACH'S CORNER
Do 5 repetitions each day.

Day:	1	2	3	4	5	(6)	(7)
	✓						

SPORTS DAY!!!

MUSIC MAKER
29. Good hand position, dynamic contrasts, and play smoothly with an even tone.

IMAGINE
that you are carrying an egg on the end of a spoon. You must carefully walk to your partner waiting across from you without dropping the egg!

FIRST EVENT

EGG & SPOON RELAY

Carefully!

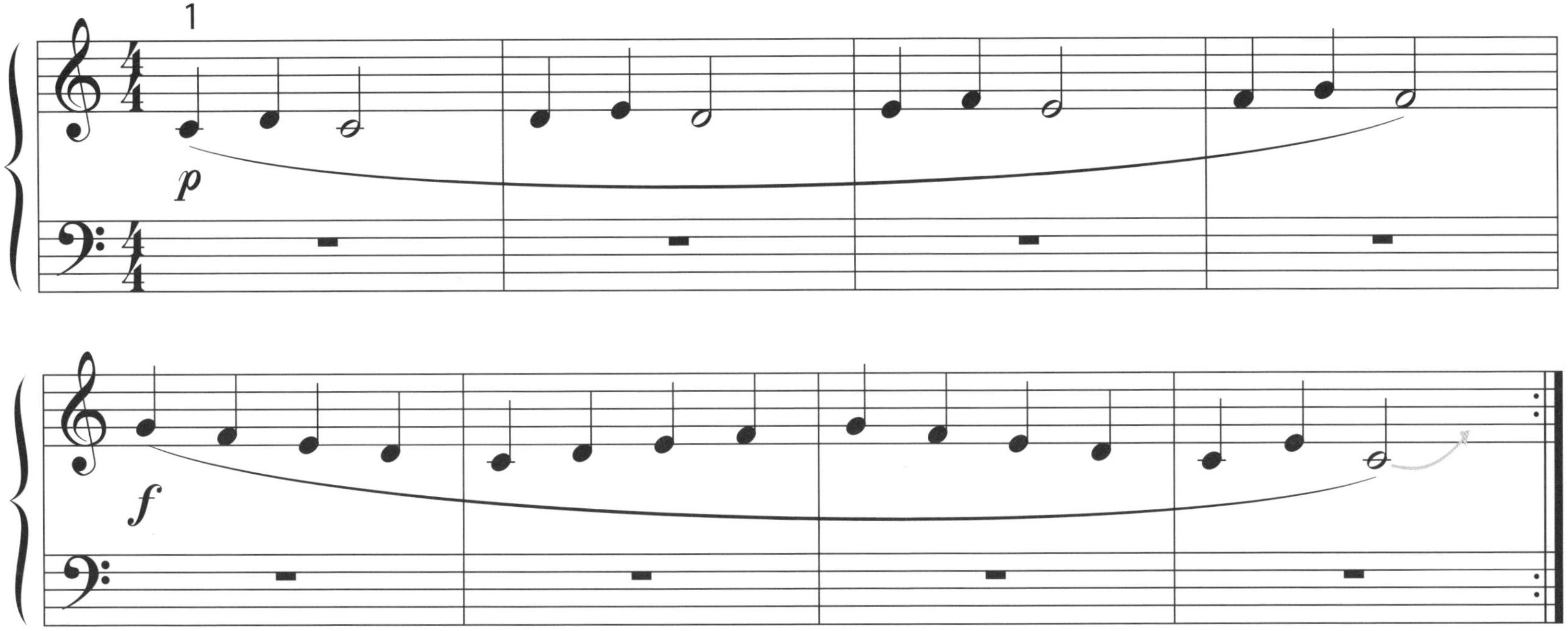

BLUE RIBBON WINNER!!!

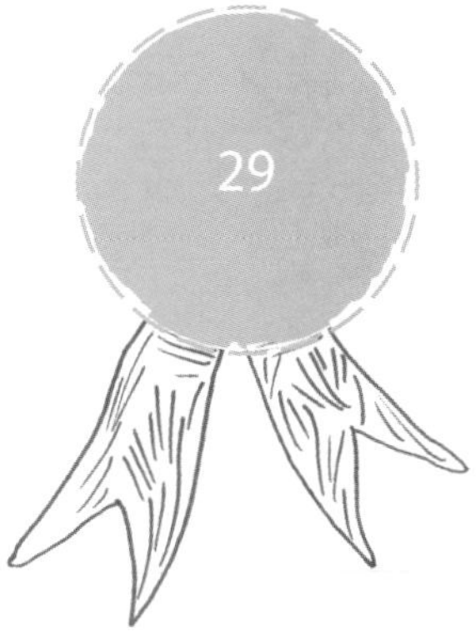

29

CORRESPONDS WITH PAGE 46 OF BEANSTALK'S LESSON BOOK PREP A.

COACH'S CORNER
Do 5 repetitions each day.

Day:	1	2	3	4	5	(6)	(7)
	✓						

SPORTS DAY!!!

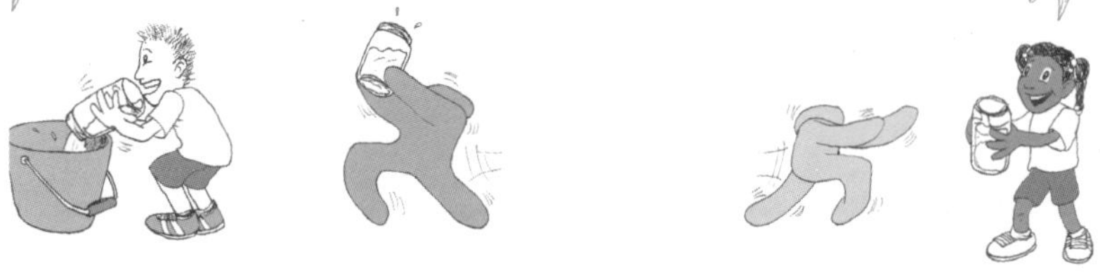

MUSIC MAKER
30. Good hand position, dynamic contrasts, and play smoothly with an even tone.

IMAGINE
you are in a water relay. Fill the jar with water, empty it, run back and get more to fill the bucket. Don't spill!

SECOND EVENT

WATER RELAY

Moderately

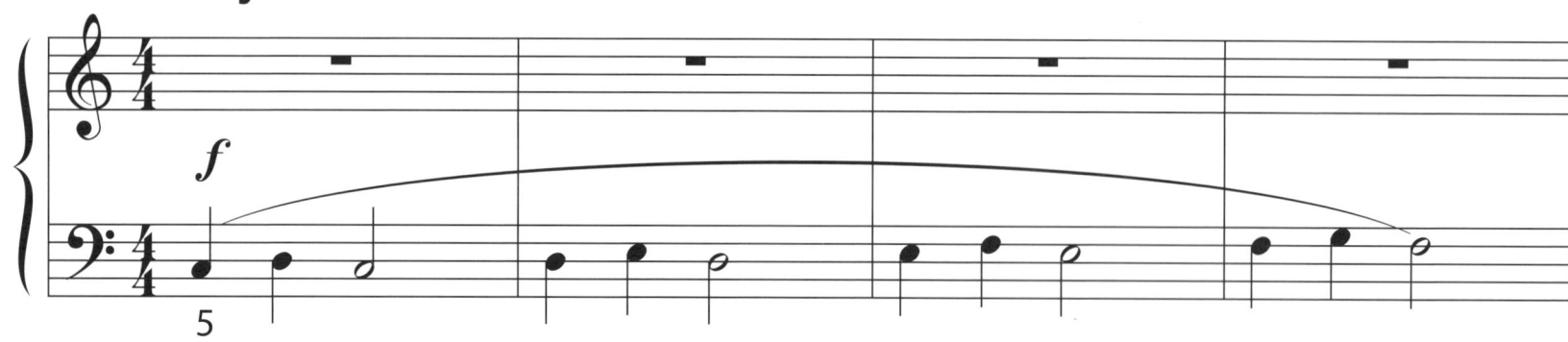

BLUE RIBBON WINNER!!!

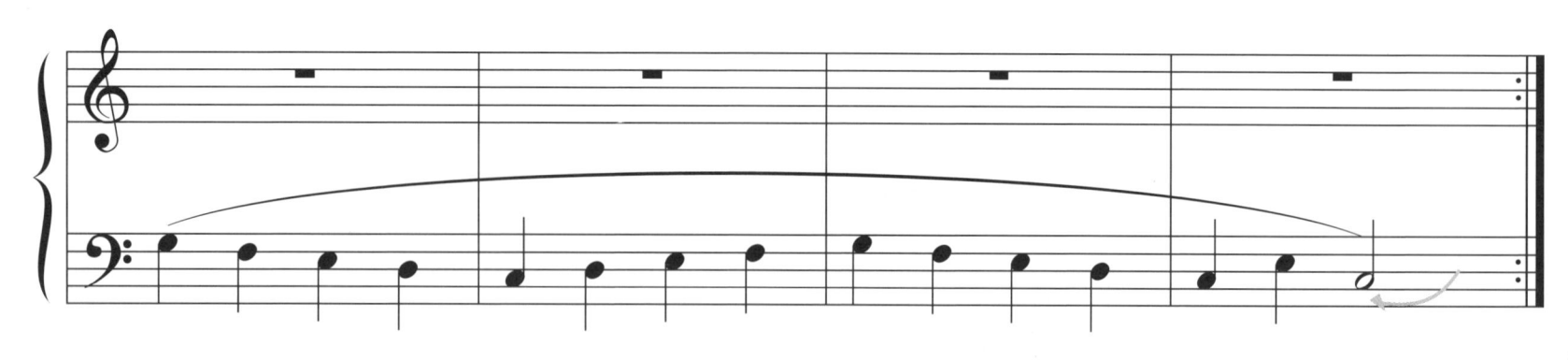

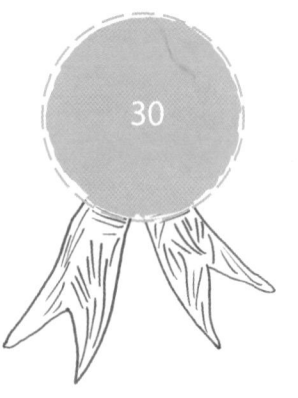

30

CORRESPONDS WITH PAGE 47 OF BEANSTALK'S LESSON BOOK PREP A.

32　　　　　　　　　　　　　　　　　　　　　　　　　　　　　　　　12461